The Snack Shop

Subtraction

Lisa Greathouse

Consultants

Chandra C. Prough, M.S.Ed.
National Board Certified
Newport-Mesa
  Unified School District

Jodene Smith, M.A.
ABC Unified School District

Publishing Credits

Dona Herweck Rice, *Editor-in-Chief*
Lee Aucoin, *Creative Director*
Chris McIntyre, M.A.Ed., *Editorial Director*
James Anderson, M.S.Ed., *Editor*
Aubrie Nielsen, M.S.Ed., *Associate Education Editor*
Neri Garcia, *Senior Designer*
Stephanie Reid, *Photo Editor*
Rachelle Cracchiolo, M.S.Ed., *Publisher*

Image Credits

Teacher Created Materials

5301 Oceanus Drive
Huntington Beach, CA 92649-1030
http://www.tcmpub.com
ISBN 978-1-4333-3434-4
© 2012 Teacher Created Materials, Inc.
BP 5028

Table of Contents

Do you like to eat snacks at a ball game?

You can go to the snack shop!

3 kids get in line.

1 kid goes to play.
Subtract!

3 − 1 = 2

3 **minus** 1 **equals** 2.
2 kids are **left**.

0 1 2 3 4 5 6 7 8 9 10

There are 5 bags of popcorn.

A girl buys 2 bags. Subtract!

$$5 - 2 = 3$$

5 minus 2 equals 3.

3 bags are left.

There are 4 lollipops.

3 lollipops are sold. Subtract!

$$4 - 3 = 1$$

4 minus 3 equals 1.
1 lollipop is left.

There are
6 hot dogs.

Kids buy 4 hot dogs. Subtract!

$$6 - 4 = 2$$

6 minus 4 equals 2.
2 hot dogs are left.

There are 7 snack bars.

5 bars are sold.
Subtract!

$$7 - 5 = 2$$

7 minus 5 equals 2.
2 snack bars are left.

There are 9 apples.

Kids buy 6 apples. Subtract!

9 – 6 = 3

9 minus 6 equals 3.
3 apples are left.

7 kids buy ice pops.

7 kids finish eating them.

Subtract!

$$7 - 7 = 0$$

7 minus 7 equals 0.

0 ice pops are left.

There are 9 bags of peanuts.

5 bags are sold.
Subtract!

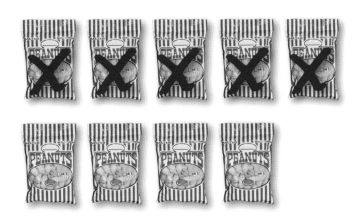

9 – 5 = 4

9 minus 5 equals 4.

4 bags are left.

10 kids buy ice cream cones.

5 kids finish their ice cream cones.

Subtract!

$$10 - 5 = 5$$

10 minus 5 equals 5.

5 ice cream cones are left.

The coach brings 10 snacks. The players eat 8 snacks.

How many snacks are left?

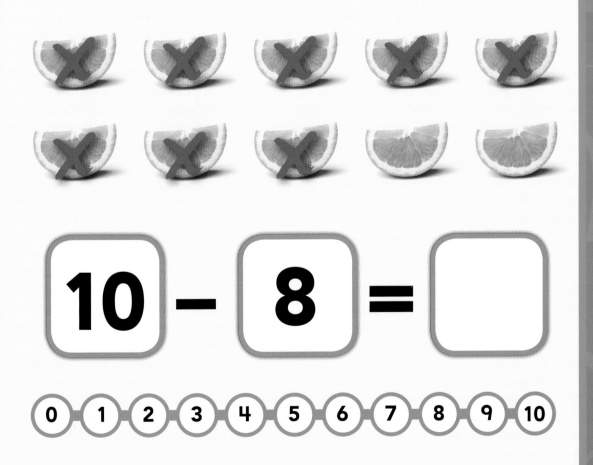

10 − 8 =

0 1 2 3 4 5 6 7 8 9 10

6 bottles of water are in the cooler.

3 bottles are sold.

How many bottles are left?

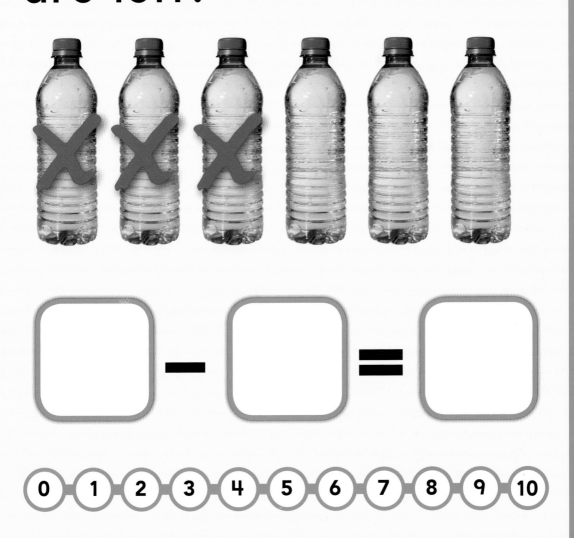

$$\boxed{} - \boxed{} = \boxed{}$$

0 1 2 3 4 5 6 7 8 9 10

The kids have 8 crackers. They eat 6 crackers. How many crackers are left?

Materials

✓ paper

✓ pencil

1 Draw 8 crackers.

2 Cross out the number of crackers the kids ate.

3 Subtract. Write a number sentence to show your answer.

Glossary

equals—has the same amount

2 = 2

left—still there

4 − 2 = 2

minus—take away

2 – 1 = 1

subtract—to take away part of an amount

2 – 1 = 1

You Try It!

Pages 24–25:
10 – 8 = 2
Two (2) snacks are left.

Pages 26–27:
6 – 3 = 3
Three (3) bottles of water are left.

Solve the Problem

Drawings may vary but should show 8 crackers with 6 crossed out. 8 – 6 = 2